HOW TO
PAY OFF YOUR MORTGAGE IN 5 YEARS

2018 EDITION

SLASH YOUR MORTGAGE WITH A PROVEN SYSTEM THE BANKS DON'T WANT YOU TO KNOW ABOUT.

ALSO BY CLAYTON & NATALI MORRIS

How to Pay Off Your Mortgage in 5 Years

> Also Available on Amazon and with other reputable book sellers.

HOW TO
PAY OFF YOUR MORTGAGE IN 5 YEARS

2018 EDITION

SLASH YOUR MORTGAGE WITH A PROVEN SYSTEM THE BANKS DON'T WANT YOU TO KNOW ABOUT.

CLAYTON MORRIS   M   NATALI MORRIS

Text copyright © 2018 Clayton Morris and Natali Morris
Cover art copyright © 2018 Clayton Morris and Natali Morris

All rights reserved.

No part of this publication may be reproduced or transmitted in any form or by any means, mechanical or electronic, including photocopying or recording, or by any information storage and retrieval system, or transmitted by email without permission in writing from the rights holders. Reviewers may quote brief passages in reviews.

Requests for authorization should be addressed to
    235 Main St. #194
    Madison NJ 07940

Interior layout and design by www.writingnights.org
Book preparation by Chad Robertson

Disclaimer and FTC Notice

While all attempts have been made to verify the information provided in this publication, neither the author nor the publisher assumes any responsibility for errors, omissions, or contrary interpretations of the subject matter herein.

This book is for entertainment purposes only. The views expressed are those of the authors alone, and should not be taken as expert instruction or commands. The reader is responsible for his or her own actions.

Adherence to all applicable laws and regulations, including international, federal, state and local governing professional licensing, business practices, advertising, and all other aspects of doing business in the US, Canada, or any other jurisdiction is the sole responsibility of the purchaser or reader.

Neither the author nor the publisher assumes any responsibility or liability whatsoever on the behalf of the purchaser or reader of these materials.

Any perceived slight of any individual or organization is purely unintentional.

CONTENTS

INTRODUCTION 1

1 – WHAT IS YOUR MORTGAGE MADE OF? 4
    What is Interest? 8
    About That Payment 16
    How Taxes and Insurance Change Your Monthly Payments 18
    There are two reasons a bank would want to bundle your taxes and insurance with your mortgage payment: 19

2 – ATTACKING YOUR MORTGAGE 23

3 – USING A HOME EQUITY LINE OF CREDIT 29
    What is a Home Equity Line of Credit? 30
    Tip 1: Shop local 34
    Tip 2: Set up your HELOC like a checking account 36
    Use Your HELOC to Slash Your Mortgage 38
    Caveats 50
    Use the Card for Everything 54
    Now About That New Tax Plan 56

4 – BORROW FROM YOUR OWN RETIREMENT ACCOUNTS 61

5 – MAKE EXTRA PRINCIPAL PAYMENTS 77

6 – CONCLUSION 85

CELEBRATE GOOD TIMES 90

THANK YOU 92

APPENDIX 94

Clayton and Natali are proud to announce the launch of our Financial Freedom Academy. If you are serious about taking control of your finances and ready to build financial freedom we invite you to join us here: www.FinancialFreedomAcademy.com

INTRODUCTION

Chances are you picked up this book because you own a house and you're tired of being a slave to your monthly mortgage payments. You're tired of working hard and never seeing any progress in paying down that massive debt. If that sounds about right, then you've come to the right place.

This book can change your life.

We know that sounds dramatic but we also know that a mortgage is dramatic. Your mortgage is the thing that keeps you slaving away for a paycheck so that the bank does not claim its stake on your home. Your mortgage can be a cage but there are many ways to escape that cage and we want to teach you to think like an escape artist! We will help you find money you didn't know you had to get rid of money you didn't even know you owed.

When you're done reading this book you'll learn the exact strategies and tactics we used to pay off multiple mortgages in a few short years, saving hundreds of thousands of dollars. It's a strategy that NO bank will tell you about!

What you're about to discover is our step-by-step system for taking your 15 or 30-year mortgage and turning it into a 5-year mortgage. Moreover, we'll teach you about the mechanisms behind the different banking products and how some are meant to keep you buried in debt for decades. It's how the banks win and you lose. Correction: it's how the banks *used to* win and you *used to* lose. But no more!

Unlike those books that promise the world and fail to deliver, what you'll get here is a blueprint that's both proven and achievable. We've got three kids and careers to manage in our house so we know how valuable time is. You don't have time to spend knee deep in finance books that leave you cross eyed. What you need—and what we will supply—is a straightforward plan that any busy person can implement to crush their primary mortgage.

We've outlined the process into a step-by-step system you can follow no matter how busy you are. In less than two months you will have everything in place to start paying off your mortgage. Obviously, results may vary depending on a variety of factors like the amount of your mortgage, your salary, credit score, etc. You'll get the blueprint but implementation is up to you.

Before we get started, we want to invite you to dream about your life if you were mortgage free. How amazing would that feel!? How free would you be to travel, not worry about grocery bills, be more generous with your money! What would you do? What would that feel like!? Keep that wishful thinking in mind as you work towards that reality by freeing yourself of the biggest expense in your life! Let's talk about how!

1
What Is Your Mortgage Made Of?

THE FIRST STEP in beating your mortgage is to understand what it's made of. In this chapter we'll break out the most important pieces without getting too deep in the weeds. The traditional mortgage is an octopus with multiple tentacles, some visible in plain sight and others hidden beneath the murky waters of the banking industry.

The first time we secured a mortgage, we assumed that the monthly payments were made up of all kinds of fees, taxes, bits and bobs. But if you look closely, it is not hard to see the anatomy of a mortgage. Let's break out some mortgage vocabulary to make sure you are crystal clear what we are talking about.

Principal: This is the amount you borrowed. You needed $100,000 to buy a home? Surely your loan statement will have a number higher than $100,000 because of closing costs, filing fees, etc.. Still $100,000 is the principal. It is the amount you asked the bank to give you.

Interest: We are going to discuss this in detail but in short: It is the amount of money you have agreed to pay in order to borrow the principal above. It is the rate of money for money. For every dollar you need to borrow, you will pay that dollar back plus an additional percentage of that dollar to the bank.

Equity: Equity is the amount of value in the house that belongs to you. If your home is worth $200,000 and you don't owe any money on it, then you have $200,000 worth of equity in the home. That value is yours. But if you owe $100,000 on that $200,000 home, your equity is $100,000. This means that if you sold the house tomorrow for $200,000, you would pay the bank back $100,000 and keep $100,000. The $100,000 that you keep is your equity.

Taxes and Insurance: You know what taxes are. You know what insurance is. (If you don't, you've picked up the wrong book.) You probably also know that when you secure a mortgage, you are obliged to pay for both taxes and insurance. Every property will be taxed and you must have insurance on your property for any lender to consider taking the risk of lending you money. Some lenders require that you add more money to your monthly payment so that they can keep it in an escrow account in order to pay the taxes and insurance for you. This adds to your monthly payment. We do NOT suggest you elect for one of these escrow accounts if given the choice. Some lenders do not give you the choice but instead require it. We will discuss this more later in this chapter.

PMI: If your lender considers your loan a little bit riskier than most, they may add an extra cost called Private Mortgage Insurance. For instance, say you can only put 10% of the purchase price on a down payment and you are asking the bank to pay for 90%. They consider you a riskier borrower. Say you have had a previous foreclosure on your credit. They consider you a riskier borrower. Your PMI may disappear once your loan value is below 80% of the property value. It may not. The point is that this is a fee. It does not pay down your principal balance. It is money you pay to the bank every month because they took a risk on loaning to you. You pay it and you will never see it again.

Those are the major components of a mortgage. Now let's really dig into the biggest beast on your mortgage statement: Interest.

WHAT IS INTEREST?

Interest is the cost of borrowing money. It is typically paid back to a lender at a regular monthly interval. Interest is based on principal, or rather is calculated based on the amount you have asked to borrow.

For the purposes of our discussion, mortgage interest rate is tied to an annual percentage rate and that means that you're paying interest every month on the unpaid balance of your loan. Still owe $100,000? Then you're paying interest on $100,000 each month even if what you initially borrowed was more.

This is important so please keep this in the back of your mind: *your interest is based on what is left on that loan*. It is calculated on your remaining balance. Therefore it stands to reason that the lower your principal balance is, the lower the amount of interest you will pay over time.

Interest on a mortgage can come in different shapes and sizes. Let's go over the most common types.

Interest-Only Loans: These are exactly what they sound like: a mortgage that has a monthly payment which includes only interest. This means that every time you make a mortgage payment, none of that money goes towards paying down your principal balance. It is a payment to the lender only. The principal balance of your loan goes untouched. So if you borrowed $100,000 and have been making interest-only payments for 5 years, your principal balance is still $100,000 because you agreed that your payments would not touch principal, whether you were aware of this or not.

This kind of loan is like the Greek tragedy of Sisyphus. He was condemned to an eternity of rolling a boulder up a hill and then watching it roll back down again. With an interest-only loan, you pay and you pay and you pay, but you are no closer to freedom because your principal balance remains the same.

Why would someone agree to these unfavorable terms? In short: because it keeps your monthly payments low. There are sometimes reasons to do this but they are beyond the scope of this book. For the most part, interest-only is not a good deal for homeowners. We have learned this the hard way.

During the 2009 mortgage collapse many homeowners had short-term balloon mortgages that were suddenly coming due. These were interest-only mortgages with a balloon note attached. A balloon note means that the principal balance will be due in full after a certain amount of time. It is a big bulk of money due at one time, which you can visualize like a balloon. These notes were popular in the early 2000s because they let homeowners get into a nice home for a low monthly payment and no money down. Unfortunately these homeowners did not understand their mortgages. At all! When they owed the full principal at the end of a short period of time and the value of the house had plummeted, they were in the weeds. Big time!

Maybe some of these homeowners had a goal to refinance these loans into amortized mortgages. We'll give them the benefit of the doubt because that sounds like an actual plan, especially given the fact that homes were appreciating at record speed back then. But it was an artificial appreciation that gave us all a real estate buzz. That buzz became a terrible hangover when home values plummeted due to the market crash. Homeowners were losing jobs and still had loans out for the entire principal balance with the clock ticking towards that balloon. It was a really sad time.

We want to help make sure this never happens to you. Most people have very little understanding of the mortgages that they sign and that gets a lot of people in trouble. Understanding the bank product you are signing up for can prevent a lot of this shock and devastation.

Amortized Loans: Amortization by definition is the paying off of a debt according to a fixed schedule. Okay, what does that mean?

When you amortize a loan, you pay for interest and principal inside of a recurring payment as you pay that loan down to $0. At the beginning of the loan, you pay a lot of interest inside that payment. As the principal balance goes down, the amount of interest you are paying goes down because it is based on a dwindling principal. You are slowly, ever so slowly, paying the loan back and working your way down to $0 owed.

We are going to do some example calculations but first we want to say something about interest rates. Interest rates on loans are based on a government-set index. So when you hear in the news that "the Fed is about to raise rates," it means that the Federal Reserve System is going to raise the base amount that lenders must use to lend money. If the Fed sets an index around 4%, your lender cannot lend to you at 2%. They are not allowed. They must lend at a rate that is based on the index. This is something none of us can really control. It often feels like it is based on government whims and that very well may be the case. All we can do as consumers is watch the index rates and try our best to secure our loans while rates are low.

Now to those calculations. Throughout this book, we are going to use a house with a $200,000 value. This house has a $150,000 mortgage at a 4% interest rate and 30 year time frame. These are what lenders refer to as "the terms." It means the amount you are borrowing, the interest rate you agree to, and the time you agree to take to pay it back. So given these terms, take a look at the first few years of an amortization schedule, detailing when each payment is due, and how much of that payment is going towards principal versus interest.

LOAN AMORTIZATION SCHEDULE

ENTER VALUES

Loan amount	$150,000.00
Annual interest rate	4.00%
Loan period in years	30
Number of payments per year	12
Start date of loan	05-06-18
Optional extra payments	

LOAN SUMMARY

Scheduled payment	$716.12
Scheduled number of payments	360
Actual number of payments	360
Total early payments	$0.00
Total interest	$107,804.26
LENDER NAME	Voldemort Savings and Loan

PMT NO	PAYMENT DATE	BEGINNING BALANCE	SCHEDULED PAYMENT	EXTRA PAYMENT	TOTAL PAYMENT	PRINCIPAL	INTEREST	ENDING BALANCE	CUMULATIVE INTEREST
1	05-06-18	$150,000.00	$716.12	$0.00	$716.12	$216.12	$500.00	$149,783.88	$500.00
2	05-07-18	$149,783.88	$716.12	$0.00	$716.12	$216.84	$499.28	$149,567.03	$999.28
3	05-08-18	$149,567.03	$716.12	$0.00	$716.12	$217.57	$498.56	$149,349.47	$1,497.84
4	05-09-18	$149,349.47	$716.12	$0.00	$716.12	$218.29	$497.83	$149,131.18	$1,995.67
5	05-10-18	$149,131.18	$716.12	$0.00	$716.12	$219.02	$497.10	$148,912.16	$2,492.77
6	05-11-18	$148,912.16	$716.12	$0.00	$716.12	$219.75	$496.37	$148,692.41	$2,989.15
7	05-12-18	$148,692.41	$716.12	$0.00	$716.12	$220.48	$495.64	$148,471.93	$3,484.79
8	05-01-19	$148,471.93	$716.12	$0.00	$716.12	$221.22	$494.91	$148,250.71	$3,979.69
9	05-02-19	$148,250.71	$716.12	$0.00	$716.12	$221.95	$494.17	$148,028.76	$4,473.86
10	05-03-19	$148,028.76	$716.12	$0.00	$716.12	$222.69	$493.43	$147,806.06	$4,967.29
11	05-04-19	$147,806.06	$716.12	$0.00	$716.12	$223.44	$492.69	$147,582.63	$5,459.98
12	05-05-19	$147,582.63	$716.12	$0.00	$716.12	$224.18	$491.94	$147,358.45	$5,951.92
13	05-06-19	$147,358.45	$716.12	$0.00	$716.12	$224.93	$491.19	$147,133.52	$6,443.12
14	05-07-19	$147,133.52	$716.12	$0.00	$716.12	$225.68	$490.45	$146,907.84	$6,933.56
15	05-08-19	$146,907.84	$716.12	$0.00	$716.12	$226.43	$489.69	$146,681.41	$7,423.25
16	05-09-19	$146,681.41	$716.12	$0.00	$716.12	$227.18	$488.94	$146,454.22	$7,912.19
17	05-10-19	$146,454.22	$716.12	$0.00	$716.12	$227.94	$488.18	$146,226.28	$8,400.37
18	05-11-19	$146,226.28	$716.12	$0.00	$716.12	$228.70	$487.42	$145,997.58	$8,887.79
19	05-12-19	$145,997.58	$716.12	$0.00	$716.12	$229.46	$486.66	$145,768.12	$9,374.45
20	05-01-20	$145,768.12	$716.12	$0.00	$716.12	$230.23	$485.89	$145,537.89	$9,860.35
21	05-02-20	$145,537.89	$716.12	$0.00	$716.12	$231.00	$485.13	$145,306.89	$10,345.47
22	05-03-20	$145,306.89	$716.12	$0.00	$716.12	$231.77	$484.36	$145,075.12	$10,829.83
23	05-04-20	$145,075.12	$716.12	$0.00	$716.12	$232.54	$483.58	$144,842.58	$11,313.41
24	05-05-20	$144,842.58	$716.12	$0.00	$716.12	$233.31	$482.81	$144,609.27	$11,796.22
25	05-06-20	$144,609.27	$716.12	$0.00	$716.12	$234.09	$482.03	$144,375.18	$12,278.25
26	05-07-20	$144,375.18	$716.12	$0.00	$716.12	$234.87	$481.25	$144,140.31	$12,759.50
27	05-08-20	$144,140.31	$716.12	$0.00	$716.12	$235.66	$480.47	$143,904.65	$13,239.97
28	05-09-20	$143,904.65	$716.12	$0.00	$716.12	$236.44	$479.68	$143,668.21	$13,719.65
29	05-10-20	$143,668.21	$716.12	$0.00	$716.12	$237.23	$478.89	$143,430.98	$14,198.55
30	05-11-20	$143,430.98	$716.12	$0.00	$716.12	$238.02	$478.10	$143,192.96	$14,676.65
31	05-12-20	$143,192.96	$716.12	$0.00	$716.12	$238.81	$477.31	$142,954.15	$15,153.96
32	05-01-21	$142,954.15	$716.12	$0.00	$716.12	$239.61	$476.51	$142,714.54	$15,630.47
33	05-02-21	$142,714.54	$716.12	$0.00	$716.12	$240.41	$475.72	$142,474.13	$16,106.19
34	05-03-21	$142,474.13	$716.12	$0.00	$716.12	$241.21	$474.91	$142,232.92	$16,581.10

Notice the monthly payment never changes but each payment has a different amount of interest, which is just the profit the bank makes from lending you that money, and principal, which is the amount you asked for to buy your house. Slowly you pay less interest over time because the interest is based on the dwindling principal balance.

This amortization schedule is a hard pill to swallow when we look under the hood. Your monthly payment amount is $716 but in early days of the loan, only $216 of that money goes towards your principal balance. The rest is payment to the bank for lending you that money.

Eventually you do pay down that principal balance after 360 monthly payments but in this time, you'll have paid over $107,000 in interest. So you paid $200,000 for the house plus $107,000 in interest for a total of $307,000 for that $200,000 house. That's a lot of money for money and a looooong time to wait to own your own house. The good news is that by the time we've colonized Mars you'll have this house paid off.

A lot of times people make themselves feel better about their mortgage by saying "At least I'm not renting! When I make that mortgage payment, it is towards something I own and so I'm not throwing that money away like I do in rent." But take another look at the amortization schedule. In the first years of your mortgage, you absolutely are **not** making payments towards something you own. Barely 30% of your mortgage payment is going towards something you own. The remaining 70% is going towards the bank. That is money you will not see again. So the rent versus mortgage rationale barely holds here.

ABOUT THAT PAYMENT

Most homeowners only pay attention to their monthly payment when they secure a mortgage. They ask themselves "Can I afford that monthly payment?" thinking very little of what that payment will amount to in the long run. This is normal primate survival type of thinking but a short sighted and very expensive mistake.

You may think "Hey, my spouse and I earn $5,000 per month in combined income and our 30 year mortgage monthly payment is $716 so we're doing great!" But so much of that hard-earned $716 is a fee to the bank that you will never see again. And if we use the above scenario, you are paying $107,000 in interest payments above the $200,000 you initially borrowed. That is $107,000 you could have done oh so much more with!

The bank is making off like a bandit. We aren't saying that they shouldn't. They assume a big risk in giving people large sums of money to purchase a home. But if you can cut down the amount of money you pay for money, shouldn't you try?

Of course you should try!!

In our family, we care much less about the monthly payment than we care about the amount we pay over the course of the loan. That is one reason why we celebrate locking in a low interest rate in our house like the birth of a new child!

When we're done with you, you're never going to look at your monthly payment the same way again. We do this by attacking principal with our payments strategically. We're getting there.

HOW TAXES AND INSURANCE CHANGE YOUR MONTHLY PAYMENTS

There is no getting around property taxes. It is simply a part of owning real estate. The same goes for insurance. Taxes and insurance are often bundled into your monthly mortgage payment. The bank takes the estimated property tax, adds it to your yearly insurance bill, and pads that number. The law allows them to collect ⅙ more than what they estimate this cost to be. They divide that number by 12 and add that to your monthly payment. Then when the tax and insurance bill comes in, your mortgage company pays it for you.

The banks spin this as a simpler alternative than getting a yearly tax bill in the mail. Isn't that so kind of them? Who needs the extra headache of having to pay my tax bill separately? Take my money and hold it for me for a while and pay my bills. Great!

Not so fast. The bank takes your extra dollars and keeps them in an escrow account. When those bills are paid, they usually send you any money that is left over in the form of a check. This is handy if you are terrible at budgeting and will not be able to pay those bills when they come but if you are terrible at budgeting, why are you reading a book like this and how have you come this far in it? Chances are that if you have picked up this book and read this far, you are pretty good with your money and are ready for advanced personal finance tricks.

THERE ARE TWO REASONS A BANK WOULD WANT TO BUNDLE YOUR TAXES AND INSURANCE WITH YOUR MORTGAGE PAYMENT:

1. You know the initialism CYA? Cover your...assets? That's what the bank is doing. If you do not pay your property taxes, the city will take priority in a lien against the house (in most states). This means that if your house has to be sold at auction or foreclosed on, the city will get paid back first before the lender. The lender has no

guarantee of ever being repaid in full. They get whatever scraps are left over from the emergency sale. The lender obviously doesn't like this option so they want to make double sure those taxes get paid!

2. They are also making money on your escrow account. The law allows the bank to lend out a portion of every dollar they are in possession of. So holding your money in an escrow account is a handy way for them to boost their business. But your escrow account is not a savings account. They do not have to pay YOU any interest whatsoever for holding this money so you could be keeping thousands of dollars in this account per year, earning ZERO% on it. Now we are not mathematicians but we do know that 0% interest is a terrible deal.

Reminder, this is YOUR money to save and earn interest on. Isn't it better to opt out of this escrow account if you are given the option? (Note: some lenders do not allow you to opt out.) Our suggestion is that you have the discipline to save this money yourself, put it in an interest-bearing account, and then you'll have some extra dough left over to ease the pain of your tax bill.

Now that you understand the various components of a mortgage, take a look at your mortgage statement. How much have you paid in interest this year? How much have you paid down principal? This may be depressing but we are going to talk about how to dwindle those numbers down in a flash.

2
Attacking Your Mortgage

WHEN IT COMES to your mortgage, public enemy number one is **interest**. Public enemy number two is **time**. This is important to keep in mind as you plan your attack.

Interest + Time = Enemies

Got it?

Good.

We've been over interest. It is simply the money you pay for money. The longer you spread those interest payments out, the more you are going to pay them to borrow this money. Why? Because the amount of interest you are paying is calculated each month based on what you have left to pay. Consider that the interest you are paying today is based on the principal balance. If you knock your principal balance down with big whacks, the time it takes to pay that mortgage back shrinks and so does the amount of interest you are paying.

We are talking about amortized interest here and amortization is an ugly beastly thing to calculate. But if you play around with an amortization calculator or spreadsheet you can see how the amount you are committed to paying in interest shrinks a TON when you put big payments in the "Extra Principal" column. This is because the amount of money you are paying for has been reduced. If you are paying 4% on $200,000, that is a much different story than paying 4% on $180,000. Duh, right?

You may have heard people say this: Oh but if you just make one extra payment per year, you can knock years off of your mortgage. This is absolutely true. But we take this principle and put it on steroids.

One extra payment per month attacks principal balance but doesn't do much to the time element. You've only knocked down a small portion of your principal balance so your interest is still being calculated on a number close to where you just were.

If you don't believe us, find any amortization calculator online or use the one built into Excel. Pretend that you've been paying your mortgage as scheduled for a year or so and then for kicks, plug in a $5,000 or $10,000 payment somewhere in year 2 or 3. Watch how the number of payments and the amount of interest paid over time plummets. Plummets! Now you know what we mean! You must attack your mortgage with big chunks of cash quickly and often.

You might be thinking, "Sounds great! But where do I find said large chunks of cash???"

One way to do this is to find a gold mine. Or a pile of cash under a mattress. Or a rich uncle. Barring these strokes of good fortune, let's look for large chunks of cash that you might not know you have access to. There are ways to find your own cash and use it to crush this major liability on your family balance sheet. We are going to go through a few of them right now but we want to be clear about our intention.

Not every strategy or banking product is for you and it is up to you to decide. If you wait for people to tell you what is best for you, you lose. Wealthy people educate themselves on the various options when it comes to personal finance and make informed and personal choices.

Our goal is for you to familiarize yourself with a variety of unorthodox choices and pick the one that works best for you.

We want to get you thinking about trading your mediocre banking products for better ones. We want to shift your thinking about money so that you do not feel like you have to do what everyone else does when it comes to mortgages, car payments, paycheck jobs, and more. Not you, dear reader. You are ready to rock a next-level game when it comes to personal finance!

3
Using A Home Equity Line Of Credit

IN THIS CHAPTER we're going to break down the benefits and mechanics of a home equity line of credit, or HELOC for short. The main thing you'll notice is how dramatically different a HELOC is from the traditional mortgage we deconstructed in Chapter 1. At the end of this chapter you'll understand how to structure your HELOC, how to find a great HELOC, and the one secret weapon that can dramatically shave years off your primary mortgage. Let's dive in!

WHAT IS A HOME EQUITY LINE OF CREDIT?

Definition: A line of credit the bank extends to you based on the equity in your home and your credit history.

Think of a HELOC like any other bank product you are used to applying for: a home loan, a car loan, a student loan. The amount you get, the interest rate you secure, and the terms of the loan are based on your finances. Do you have good credit? Do you already have a lot of debt? Do you have a good job? All of these are factored into the final loan terms.

So you go to your bank and say, "I'd like to apply for a home equity line of credit please." Be sure to say please.

The banker will hand you an application. The application will ask you about all of the above questions and then ask for proof of your answers by way of bank statements, pay stubs, drivers licenses, etc. Then the bank will run your credit. Obviously the higher the better.

Some good numbers to aim for here are a credit score of 660 or above, and a debt-to-income ratio of 45% or lower. This means that for all of the income you bring home, 45% or less of it goes to paying off debt. If too much of your paycheck is spoken for in debt payments, banks don't want anything to do with you. Who wants to get at the back of the line for creditors if they know that they won't get paid back? Many banks will look at anything under 36% debt as highly favorable. Make sure you know your number before you apply so you won't be embarrassed.

Now remember that your HELOC is based on the equity you own in your home. The equity is based on the amount your home is worth in relation to the amount you owe. The bank offers to lend you a percentage of your equity. More about that later. What you need to know for starters is that in order to determine your home equity, the bank will need to appraise your home so they know what it is worth. They don't take your word for it. Everyone thinks they have the best house in the neighborhood. The bank needs proof. They want to know what the house could be sold for if you put it on the market today. Current market value.

The bank will assign an appraiser to your home. Sometimes they pay for this appraisal and sometimes they make you pay for it. Ask them about this when you apply. We have never paid for the appraisal on my HELOCs. Try to make sure you don't either.

Now that the bank has an appraisal that they trust, they can determine your equity. Let's stick with our scenario of a $200,000 house. The bank appraiser confirms that this is the current market value. Let's say that you still owe $150,000 on this house so your equity is

$50,000.

A bank will give you a loan based on this equity because that equity is as good as cash if the home were sold. They will **not** give you a loan based on the entire value of the house. That would be taking out debt on your debt and even though this is America, we don't take debt quite that far. Your HELOC will be a percentage of the $50,000 equity that you would get out of your home sale. Most commonly, the loan will be between 70-90% of that equity. For simplicity sake let's assume an 80% loan of your $50,000 equity, which is $40,000.

So if all goes well, you've been approved for a $40,000 HELOC. Sweet! Now what?

Let's start with terms. If your credit is good and your debt is low, you can demand some great terms. Many banks offer a low introductory rate for the first year. Our bank gave us a 1.99% interest rate for the first year in 2015 when rates were quite low. These terms are based on a lot of things though. When the market is good, interest rates are low, interest rates on HELOCs are good. When the market changes, interest rates can go up.

You know you're an adult when you get excited about things like low interest rates.

The typical HELOC is a 10 or 15 year loan. This is negotiable. You will make a monthly payment on this loan and you can choose interest-only or an amortized payment which will knock down the principal of the loan. Our HELOCs are interest-only and we will explain that more later.

For the purposes of this book, we are going to use a HELOC with a 3% interest rate for 15 years as an example.

Before we get to what you do with that money, let's first discuss two more tips about shopping for your HELOC.

TIP 1: SHOP LOCAL

We're not being idyllic here. Local banks can usually do

much more for you than the large national chains can. We have a great relationship with our local bankers. They often waive bank fees for us with a few keystrokes just because we are sitting at their desks. They go to bat for us if the corporate office offers us terms we are not thrilled about. They give us lots of free pens. They tolerate our children playing the spin-until-you-fall-over game on their office chairs. Mostly.

Local bankers also have a better understanding of your property value since they live in the same town. A national chain with a call center in another time zone will not be able to get an accurate sense of your home value. A banker that lives in your community will be much more comfortable in assessing your equity based on current market conditions.

Local banks usually have great incentives for you as well. They can't compete with the big chains without them. So look for low introductory interest rates, free checking and savings accounts, no-fee credit cards, and more.

Of course there are drawbacks to using a local bank. They won't have nearly as many ATMs and their website and online banking will never be as robust as a Bank of America or Wells Fargo. That's just the way it goes. Our preference is to go without these bells and whistles for the low rates and fees.

Our advice is to shop around between 3-4 banks, a few local and a few chains. See what each one can do for you and choose the most attractive player. What's that commercial that says that when banks compete, you win? It was probably a large banking corporation ironically enough but they were right!

TIP 2: SET UP YOUR HELOC LIKE A CHECKING ACCOUNT

Ask your bank if your HELOC can receive direct deposit. It should be easy to do but our banker did not know that a HELOC could do that until we actually did it. Here is how.

A HELOC really does work like a checking account. Think about it, they've just extended you $40,000 worth of credit. You don't have to use it. It's up to you. They did not give you $40,000. They gave you the *option* to use $40,000.

How do you use it? With an account worth $40,000. You get an account number, a routing number, and possibly some checks and a debit card. The HELOC has a 0 balance when you open it. Say you spend $1,000. Now the HELOC has a $1,000 balance and a $39,000 line of credit. You spend another $1,000. Now the HELOC has a $2,000 balance and a $38,000 line of credit. The balance is what you have used of your original allotment.

So how do you pay that $2,000 back? We do this with direct deposit of the paycheck from our day jobs. Each week the entire paycheck goes into the HELOC to keep that balance moving back to 0. We'll explain more later but just know that keeping your HELOC in check and your money going exactly where you want it is much easier when your paycheck is filtered through your HELOC.

Our bank calls to verify each transaction out of our HELOC. This is a nice service to make sure that there is no fraud but can be kind of annoying if you use your HELOC for small purchases. So don't use it to buy a coffee. Use it for large purchases only. We're about to get into that right now so buckle up.

USE YOUR HELOC TO SLASH YOUR MORTGAGE

Sticking with our example of the $40,000 HELOC, imagine now that you put that entire chunk of money onto your $150,000 principal balance. Important tactical note: you must mark your payments as "**principal only**." We've had banks try to take interest and regular payments out of those extra payments and we've had to send Natali in with her Mommy-Means-Business face to tell them that they had just better put that money towards the principal balance or else! Insert angry red emoji face here.

Since time is an important element on an amortization schedule, let's hypothetically say that we are in the first year of our mortgage. Of course you will most likely not do this on the first payment of a brand new mortgage because you wouldn't even have had time to secure a HELOC at the same time as your mortgage but we are going to try to keep our numbers even so let's just take that $40,000 and see what it would do to a $150,000 loan.

Imagine that HELOC like a weapon. Swing it at your mortgage. Go!

When you put a $40,000 chunk down on a $150,000 balance, you will see that the amount of interest you were scheduled to pay the bank has been reduced by $63,134.78. Whaaaaaat? You are now scheduled to pay $44,669.48 in total interest over the life of your loan. You were originally scheduled to pay $107,804.26 in interest. Doesn't it feel good just looking at the difference!

Also take a look at the number of payments on your amortization schedule. You agreed to 360 payments or 30 years. With that big swing at principal, you are now scheduled for 216 payments. That is a whole 144 fewer payments or 12 whole years!

Okay but wait! You started with a liability of $150,000. But now you owe $40,000 to the HELOC and $110,000 to the principal mortgage, which is still $150,000. True! But you've transferred nearly one third of your debt into a lower-interest loan!

Assuming you pay the HELOC back according to the schedule you agreed upon, the overall interest on the $40,000 loan is $18,000 if you choose an interest-only HELOC. If you choose an amortized HELOC it is even less but we are going to assume an interest-only HELOC and we'll explain why later.

So, if you add that $18,000 to your new overall interest on your mortgage of $44,669.48, you have $62,669.48. That means you are scheduled to pay $62,669.48 on the $150,000 liability rather than the $107,804.26 you were originally set to pay. You are saving $45,134.78. Do we have your attention now??

Remember, you've taken a $40,000 liability and strapped it to a lower-interest bank product and grade school math tells us that higher interest>lower interest so by transitive property, owning the HELOC $40,000 is far better than owning the primary mortgage $40,000!

Also remember that the HELOC is paid back in simple interest rather than amortized interest. Up until this point we've been talking about amortized interest. Simple interest is determined by multiplying the daily interest-rate by the principal balance by the number of days that have elapsed between the payments you've made.

More simply (pun intended), simple interest is based on what you have borrowed and does not change depending on what is left on the loan. It is based on what you borrowed and agreed upon. So you are better off paying a loan with simple interest and knocking off the loan with amortized interest.

In fact, our general game plan is to take that HELOC and use it like a weapon. We swing it at every loan that we don't like in life: high-interest credit card balances, car loans, home loans. The HELOC is an awesome product. We want to switch it out for any bank products we have that are not awesome.

Allow us to illustrate with a visual that might help you make decisions about your HELOC.

Our kids love the teeter totter at the playground. Some call it a seesaw. You know this childhood game: one goes up and the other comes crashing down. One is lighter one is heavier. Paying down your primary mortgage is a lot like the teeter totter. You put your two bank products on either side of the teeter totter. Which one is heavier, meaning costs you more? Which one is lighter, meaning costs you less? You want to destroy the heaviest one with the lightest one. Once you've done that, put your next heavy bank product on the opposing end and destroy that too. This is the true definition of leverage and it is a game the wealthy know how to play all too well!

Let's turn our attention to the side of the teeter totter that has the HELOC. You want that loan paid off of course. How do we do that?

You could make payments to the HELOC every month with as much money as you can save up from your income. That's one way, sure. But we have another ninja trick way that works even better! Here's how it goes:

You tell your employer to put your entire paycheck into the HELOC as a direct deposit. Your HELOC is a bank account just like your checking account so why the heck not? So that HELOC gets ALL of your money that you make every month. And of course the balance will go down, down, down because you are doing this.

Wait, you say, how will I buy groceries? Pay my actual mortgage bill? Cell phone bill? Etc.!?

Good question! You pay it out of the HELOC. And if you spend less money than you made this month, the remaining balance will sit in the HELOC and dwindle that balance down to 0 before you know it.

Let's run a scenario to show what we mean. You have a $40,000 HELOC. You put $40,000 on your mortgage principal so that HELOC has a $40,000 balance. You make $10,000 per month. You direct deposit all of that $10,000 into your HELOC so the HELOC now has a $30,000 balance.

Now, your monthly expenses are $8,000. You pay for them out of the HELOC so now your principal balance is $38,000. So in one month, you have paid your HELOC down by $2,000. Do this WHOLE THING

OVER next month and the HELOC balance is now $36,000. Do this for 18 months and your HELOC is down to 0!

But in 18 months, your introductory interest rate on that HELOC may be pretty high. Good point but the equity in your house is higher now, right? Renegotiate a new HELOC! Find a new bank! Go shopping for a more awesome bank product or ask your bank to re-negotiate the one you've got.

Remember the HELOC was based on your equity of $50,000. But now you have equity of $90,000 so you are eligible for more money at a new low rate. So now you can do the same thing over again! Do it!

Let's continue to play this out because it is exciting. You have secured a HELOC based on your new equity of $90,000.00. Let's say it is for $70,000.00 and we are now 20 months into the mortgage. Your remaining principal balance on the primary mortgage is $102,927.10 because in addition to working on that

HELOC, you've been paying your regularly-scheduled payments of $716.12 too.

You swing that $70,000 at the $102,927.10 principal balance. Now the amount you are set to pay in total interest on the primary mortgage is $10,399.58. Hold that up against the $107,000 you were originally set to pay and you've saved yourself $97,404 in interest overall! You have also reduced the number of payments on this house to 71 from 360. That is over 24 years in mortgage payments you will not be making my friend!

Now you have to attack that $70,000. You pay it back $2,000 per month like we did the $40,000 HELOC. This new HELOC is back to 0 in 35 months or a little under 3 years. So now in approximately 5 years, you have paid off $110,000 of your principal mortgage and now have a $10,000 balance! Holy moly!!

So you take out a new HELOC for up to $150,000.00 because you have a ton of equity to use. But you only need $10,000 because that is all that is left on your primary mortgage. In month 56 of your mortgage, you use the HELOC to pay off the remaining $10,717.65. Now you have NO primary mortgage and just $10,000 to pay back on the HELOC. This takes you 5 months at your $2,000 per month schedule.

You have now paid $10,140 in total interest on that primary mortgage and you paid it off in 56 payments or just under 5 years. Compare that to the $107,000 and 30 years that you had originally agreed to. Much, much, much better!

How about that HELOC interest. When you took out the first loan for $40,000, you were scheduled to pay $18,000 in interest over 15 years. But you didn't pay it back in 15 years. You paid it back in less than 2 years. That is because you are constantly putting your paycheck towards the principal balance. That is why we selected the interest-only HELOC. We want the lowest monthly payment on that HELOC because we are paying it down at super speed. The amortization of the loan doesn't really matter.

The monthly payment on an interest-only $40,000 HELOC at 3% for 15 years is $100. Consider this fee the cost of doing this strategy. Even if you add that back into our numbers, you come out way ahead. If you choose an amortized HELOC, the monthly payment is $276.23. Why waste that extra money when you are going to accelerate this HELOC payoff anyway?

Allow us to summarize these numbers below.

	Original Mortgage	Accelerated Mortgage	HELOC
Balance	$150,000.00	$110,000.00	$40,000.00
Total Interest Scheduled To Be Paid	$107,804.16	$44,669.48	$18,000.00
Interest Saved	$0	$63,134.78	$15,600.00
Total Number of Payments	360	216	20
Number of Payments Saved	0	144	160

NOTE: Payments on an interest-only HELOC for $40,000 at 3% is $100 per month. This means the scheduled amount of interest on that loan is $18,000.00. By paying it off in two years, we pay only $2,400 in interest, saving us $15,600.00 in overall interest.

HELOC #2: $70,000.00, 21 months into mortgage.

	Original Mortgage	Accelerated Mortgage	HELOC
Balance	$102,927.10	$32,554.07	$70,000.00
Total Interest Scheduled To Be Paid	$44,669.48	$10,339.58	$31,500.00
Overall Interest Saved	$0	$97,404.68	$25,375.00
Total Number of Payments	216	216	35
Number of Payments Saved	0	289	145

NOTE: Payments on an interest-only HELOC for $70,000 at 3% is $175 per month. This means the scheduled amount of interest on that loan is $31,500. By paying it off in two years, we pay only $6,125 in interest, saving us $25,375.00.

HELOC #3: $70,000.00, 56 months into mortgage.

	Original Mortgage	Accelerated Mortgage	HELOC
Balance	$10,717.65	10,717.65	10,717.65
Total Interest Scheduled To Be Paid	$10,399.00	$10,140.14	$133.95
Interest Saved	$0	$97,664.02	$4,688.05
Total Number of Payments	71	56	5
Number of Payments Saved	0	304	175

NOTE: Payments on an interest-only HELOC for $10,717 at 3% is $26.79 per month. This means the scheduled amount of interest on that loan is $4,822.20. By paying it off in two years, we pay only $133, saving us $25,375.00

CAVEATS

There are two caveats we must make based on the 2018 tax changes and your personal budgeting. First about budgeting.

Keep in mind that the key here is that you spend less than you make every single month. You have to have money left at the end of the month, not month left at the end of the money. Every dollar you do not spend pays down your HELOC so that you can pay down your mortgage faster and faster.

Earlier we asked you to shop around for a bank that will let you use your home-equity line of credit as a checking account complete with a debit card, checkbook, and the ability to make deposits. I'm willing to bet that every month your normal checking account has a few hundred dollars left over just sitting there doing nothing. That money is not in the stock market, it's not in your 401(k). It's just sitting there. With our new strategy you're going to use that monthly leftover cash like a heat seeking missile to pay down our home-equity line of credit.

Now about those daily expenses like your daily latte

or commuter train pass. Can you pay for those from your HELOC? You can but it can get tedious. Instead, we recommend paying for EVERYTHING with a low-interest, high-rewards credit card. Then you pay this credit card IN FULL every month with your HELOC account. This way the bank does not call you to authorize every purchase out of your HELOC like our bank does. It gets annoying fast. But also, you rack up points on every purchase with the card of your choice. Shop around for the best card you can get on Bankrate.com. We have paid for almost all of our travel using this strategy because we spend everything on the card and reap all the benefits. It's awesome!

There are other benefits of using a credit card for your expenses:

1. The security: Debit cards don't offer the same level of security as a credit card. Every transaction is protected by Visa, MasterCard, or American Express. Erroneous transactions can easily be removed from your account if you notice some foul play. Additionally these cards offer car insurance and other protections when you use their services. You don't get that with an ATM card.

2. The Rewards: Disney vacations, airline miles, cash back, you name it, there's a card that will make you happy with the rewards offering! Natali was particularly joyous about the new Amazon Chase Visa that offers 5% cash back for purchases at Whole Foods and Amazon. Which is why our neighbor boy went as an Amazon Prime box for Halloween.

3. Improved Credit Score: An ancillary benefit of using a credit card and paying it off every month is that you're dramatically improving your credit score. Banks love to see that you are using their services and paying them back on time. Having an improved credit score will also help you when you want to renegotiate the terms of your

HELOC at a future date. You may even get a lower interest rate thanks to your improved credit score.

USE THE CARD FOR EVERYTHING

Our ATM cards are only used when we need cash. For everything else, we use our credit cards. Trips to Home Depot, Netflix, breakfast at the diner, and dry cleaning. You name it and it goes on the credit card. Remember that all of these transactions get paid off each month directly out of the HELOC. You might still get a phone call from the bank to verify the transaction but one phone call is better than 30.

Does this take discipline? Of course it does! This entire strategy takes discipline but this is an advanced personal finance technique and you would not have made it this far in a book like this if you were not a disciplined person.

Part of this discipline is to set a goal to reduce your monthly expenses as much as possible. You don't have to go crazy but if you eat out six times a month try to cut that down to just four. That might save you $150 a month and because that additional cash is sitting in your HELOC account it's reducing your overall HELOC balance. We set a goal to eat meals at home more often and that brought down our monthly expenses.

Be honest with yourself and budget for all of your monthly expenses. Taking a few hours and tallying up every monthly item you spend can be eye opening. When we did this, we discovered a few internet subscription services that we were paying for that we'd totally forgotten and were no longer using. That extra $60 a month helped pay off our HELOC. By making a few small changes you will more quickly slice and dice your mortgage.

Remember, every dollar you don't spend helps pay down your HELOC, which helps pay down your mortgage. That is a powerful motivator not to overspend because it brings you that much closer to being free of the biggest loan in your name, your mortgage! The biggest monkey on your back, we're willing to bet!

NOW ABOUT THAT NEW TAX PLAN

In 2018 the Republican-led congress passed a sweeping new tax law that disallows interest from a HELOC to be written off on state and federal taxes. This is a bit of a bummer for this strategy. The interest you pay to your primary mortgage is a deduction. The interest you pay to the HELOC now is not. There are some ways to deduct this interest but using it to pay down your primary mortgage is not one of them.

So will this still work? The answer is: It depends. Let's use our scenario to figure this out. Pretend we are in year 1 of owning this home. We were scheduled to pay $107,804.26 in interest this year for our primary mortgage. But in January, we took out a HELOC and put $40,000 towards our primary mortgage. Now we will pay $2,400 in non-tax deductible interest to the

HELOC and $44,669.58 in tax deductible interest to the primary mortgage. But we are saving overall $63,135.78 in life-long interest on the HELOC. Even if you add back that $2,400 that you pay to the HELOC, you are still making out like a bandit on the interest schedule.

Does it hurt in this year's taxes? Only a little because you are still making regularly-scheduled payments to your primary mortgage with interest included in those payments. You are still getting the tax advantage on those. You are just not getting the tax advantage of the interest on the HELOC, which is admittedly much less anyway.

So yes this still works out but you have to think of that $2,400 HELOC interest payment as an added expense. It stinks. If you are in a tax situation where you NEED every deduction you can get your hands on, put this plan on the back burner. But if you can stomach the interest expense, then don't throw out the baby with the bath water. This plan still can work for you! Talk to your tax planner about it!

4

Borrow From Your Own Retirement Accounts

WE HAVE TO hand it to the investment banks. They really have succeeded in marketing the 401(k) as the holy grail of savings tools. They have most people so brainwashed that some act like they might go to federal prison if they even *think* about touching it. But let us assure you: your 401(k) money is more accessible than you think it is.

At best, the 401(k) is a good product. It is not a great product. Our favorite tax accountant Tom Wheelwright, author of *Tax-Free Wealth: How to Build Massive Wealth by Permanently Lowering Your Taxes*, calls the 401(k) a way for you to partner with the government to invest in the stock market. When you really learn to evaluate financial products, you will not be so impressed with the 401(k).

Most 401(k)s have very high fees paid to the big banks that host them. Most of them have very limited choices as to what you invest them in and most of them are based on the volatile stock market. Most of them are traditional 401(k)s that the government taxes when you hit retirement age, therefore not taxing the seed— the money you put into it when you were working, but rather taxing the crop—the amount that money has grown into.

We know the commercials would have you believe that a very good looking silver fox of a man is about to live out his retirement in style on his 401(k) but we have never met a family that has actually done this. That is because the average 401(k) balance at retirement age hovers around $90,000.

The numbers here will depress you. Let's say you retire at 59½, which is when your 401(k) plan becomes available to you without a withdrawal penalty. Now figure that the government is still going to tax your withdrawals at your current tax rate so that $90,000 is going to get a nice 25% reduction at best.

Let's pretend we could magically avoid taxes. Even without that taxation, how long can you live on $90,000? The average American salary hovers around $80,000. So assuming you are living on an annual budget of something similar, your 401(k) will buy you little more than one year in living. And then what? And then you better die? That is not a plan and if it is, it's a morbid one.

Maybe you've got a Roth 401(k). That's better, to be sure, because it means that you have contributed post-tax dollars, instead of pre-tax dollars. This means that the government has taxed the seed and not the crop so when you withdraw, you are withdrawing tax-free. That's nice but it is still $90,000 and we've seen how far that can go already. How long into your retirement will $90,000 get you? We plan to travel the world and drink expensive wine and $90,000 will simply not allow for that!

So now that we've dumped all kinds of wet blankets on your 401(k) rainbow, what are you to do with the one you've got? Use it better!

You may not know this but you are allowed to take a LOAN out of your 401(k) to yourself. This is not a withdrawal. It is a loan! That means the custodian is going to make you put it back. When we refer to the custodian, we mean the company that holds the 401(k) like Fidelity or Goldman Sachs.

Most custodians allow you to loan yourself up to 50% of what is in there or $50,000 at a time, whichever is lesser. That means that they take the money that is currently there, probably invested in some mutual fund, sell off $50,000 of the asset, and give you $50,000. It is actually pretty simple. In our Fidelity 401(k), it was a matter of about 4 mouse clicks and the money arrived in our checking account within 3-5 business days.

You will set the interest rate of the loan but the interest payments you make go to YOUR 401(k) and not the bank. After all, you are the lender of your own money. You also set the terms of the payback over a set number of months.

Even better: Is this interest being paid to a bank? No it is not! It is being paid to YOU! An account that you own!

So let's say you borrowed $40,000 from your 401(k) and put it towards a principal balance on your

$150,000 mortgage. Now you have saved the same amount of money in interest payments to the bank but you have begun to EARN interest as a lender.

Some people like to come back at us on Twitter with quips about losing out on the earnings that money would have been invested in had you left it alone. Our response to that: So what? When Clayton left his job during a stock market boom in 2017, he called Fidelity to roll his 401(k) into a self-directed IRA. The representative that took the call said,

"Are you sure you want to do that? We can roll this money into an IRA here and you can keep the same funds you already have. These funds are performing pretty well at 2%!"

TWO percent? Clayton politely declined but we had a good laugh over this later. You want to leave your 401(k) money alone because it is making 2%? Rather than make 4% in interest from yourself? If this is your argument, maybe you need to revisit 2nd grade math which taught us that 4%>2%.

But if you see the myopic nature of this argument, then the light is going on in your head! You take that $40,000, you save yourself a boatload of interest and time on your mortgage, and you make at least 4% back in the 401(k) as the lender.

Another silver lining: the amount you pay yourself in interest does not go towards your annual contribution limit. This means that if you continue to contribute the $16,500 per year that is allowed by law, you could be contributing more because those interest payments don't count towards your contribution limits so you are boosting that account.

Could you pay yourself more interest? In some cases, sure. Check with your custodian. You don't want to go too crazy with interest to yourself for two reasons.

1. You don't want to trigger an audit because you are charging yourself usury loans. Usury means that

the loan is unfairly beneficial to the lender because the interest rates are so much higher than normal.
2. These payments will be automatically deducted from your paycheck and you have to be sure you can budget for that.

Which brings us to an important point: this loan will reduce the amount of your paycheck. You will take home less because the loan payment is automatic. You have to do the math to figure out what you can afford. Be aggressive and conservative at the same time. Remember, this payment is still YOUR money. But it is money you are taking away from your monthly take-home pay for a short amount of time.

So let's play this scenario out so you see how it works. We still have the same $150,000 liability at 4% interest rate to the bank. You borrow $40,000 from your 401(k) and decide you want to pay that 4% interest rate to yourself and not the bank. You swing that $40,000 towards your $150,000 mortgage like a sledgehammer. Boom! You've now saved yourself $63,134.78 in interest payments and 144 payments, just like before. But the new interest you are paying to your 401(k) loan? Well it's not really an expense is it? It's a payment to your own Performing Asset! You are now set to pay 4% in interest on that $40,000 but to yourself! Look at it this way:

	Original Mortgage	Mortgage + $40,000 401(k) Loan
Interest To Pay	$107,804.26	$44,669.58 + $1,687.93 = $46,357.41
Interest You Earn	$0	$1,687.83
Number of Payments	360	216
Number of Payments Saved	0	144 (12 years!)
Interest Saved	$0	$61,446.85

Now let's see how your repayment plan goes. Let's say you decided to pay that $40,000 back over the course of 2 years at 4% interest. This means you owe yourself $1,737.00 per month. That sounds like a hefty new liability you're agreeing to but we are planning an aggressive schedule here. Plus, remember in the previous chapter we were assuming that you could find an extra $2,000 in your budget at the end of every month. If this is not realistic for you, choose a number that is. We're trying to plan for an aggressive payoff schedule so let's continue to use these numbers.

Remember, you could always lower your interest rate or increase the lifespan of the loan to make this more manageable. Giving yourself 4 years would lower the monthly payment to $903 if that feels better. Play with an online loan calculator to figure out what you can swing but let's pretend that you can afford to be aggressive and pay that $40,000 loan back to yourself in two years. This means that you will have made $1,687.93 in interest as the lender off of yourself. So cool!

Let's continue to play these numbers out until the

end of the mortgage. After two years, you have paid back the 401(k) loan and are ready to take out another one. Your custodian may make you wait a few months depending on the calendar year or other rules but let's pretend our custodian doesn't have rules like that. We can take out another loan and this time we are going to take $50,000.00. It is month 25 and our principal balance on the mortgage is $101,427.49. We put a $50,000 principal payment and bam! We are now scheduled to pay only $16,287.79 in total interest and will only make 107 payments. This is a savings of over $90,000 in interest and 253 mortgage payments!

You are still paying the 401(k) loan back at the same terms: 2 years at 4% for a $1,737.00 monthly payment. So let's look at how that plays out below.

	Original Mortgage	Mortgage + $40,000 401(k) Loan #1	Mortgage + $40,000 401(k) Loan #2
Interest To Pay	$107,804.26	$44,669.58 + $1,687.93 = $46,357.41	$16,287.79 + $1,687.93 = $17,975.72

	Original Mortgage	Mortgage + $40,000 401(k) Loan #1	Mortgage + $40,000 401(k) Loan #2
Interest You Earn	$0	$1,687.83	$1,687.83 + $1,687.83 = $3,375.86
Number of Payments	360	216	107
Number of Payment Saved	0	144	253 (21 years!)
Interest Saved	$0	$61,446.85	$89.828.54

Let's keep going!

It takes us two years to pay back that 401(k) loan and now we are in month 50 of our mortgage and our principal balance is $37,431.69. We can knock that out in one fell swoop and eliminate our mortgage and now ONLY have our own loan to ourselves to pay off! So let's take a 401(k) loan for only $37,431.69. We get that money, put it towards the payoff of our mortgage and look at the numbers! We will now have only paid $12,646.48 in overall interest on the mortgage. Compare that to the $107,804.26 we had committed to paying when we signed for the mortgage and you will see that you saved yourself $95,157.78 in interest payments! And how many payments did you make? Not 360 like you had originally committed to. Nope! You made 50 payments total, saving yourself 310 payments or 25 years in mortgage payments! Forgettaboutit!

As for the loan you are making to yourself from the 401(k), the payments are $1,625.47 and the overall interest made to yourself is $1,579.55.

	Original Mortgage	Mortgage + $40,000 401(k) Loan #1	Mortgage + $40,000 401(k) Loan #2	Mortgage + $40,000 401(k) Loan #3
Interest To Pay	$107,804.26	$44,669.58 + $1,687.93 = $46,357.41	$16,287.79 + $1,687.93 = $17,975.72	$12,646.48 + $1,687.93 +
Interest You Earn	$0	$1,687.83	$1,687.83 + $1,687.83 =	$0
Number of Payments	360	216	107	50
Number of Payment Saved	0	144	253 (21 years!)	310 (25 years!)
Interest Saved	$0	$61,446.85	$89,828.54	$91,890.30

Note that since you no longer have a mortgage payment this time around, you could extend the life of your 401(k) loan for a few more years to lower the payment to give yourself a break. Then again, you don't have a mortgage payment now so that loan repayment shouldn't be that hard.

Now this was an aggressive schedule to pay off a mortgage in less than 5 years but it can be done! You just have to plug your own numbers in and see what you can do.

You can do this with any debt really. It doesn't have to be a mortgage payment. If we had expensive student loan debt, we'd definitely employ this strategy! Not-great interest rate on a car? Do this! Credit card debt weighing you down at 15%? DEFINITELY do this! Don't ever pay 15% for money. Never! Use money at your disposal and get rid of any unfavorable debt you can!

We have also used this strategy to buy investment real estate. That means we have used ourselves as the lender to buy Performing Assets. The rental income was used to repay the loan and we ended up cash flowing every single month. This is a strategy beyond the scope of this book but what we'd like you to take away is the fact that your money does not have to hang out in a mediocre 401(k) when it could be working for you so efficiently.

5
Make Extra Principal Payments

THE STRATEGIES SUGGESTED in previous chapters assume that you have some assets to your name such as equity in your home and a 401(k). But what if you don't? Can you go the old "pay extra to principal" route?

Of course you can!

Every dollar you pay the bank in extra principal reduces your overall interest and time burden. You absolutely can knock this out in small chunks. The advantage to using the ways we have thus far suggested is that you are attacking time AND interest together. But if you can only afford to tackle interest in small but mighty swings, it counts!

Get used to playing with numbers in amortization spreadsheets. You can't really do this online because an online amortization calculator will not take into account historical principal payments. You have to find one that allows you to put hypothetical payments into specific months. For instance see these charts:

LOAN AMORTIZATION SCHEDULE

ENTER VALUES		LOAN SUMMARY	
Loan amount	$150,000.00	Scheduled payment	$716.12
Annual interest rate	4.00%	Scheduled number of payments	360
Loan period in years	30	Actual number of payments	336
Number of payments per year	12	Total early payments	$6,000.00
Start date of loan	05-06-18	Total interest	$96,514.06
Optional extra payments		LENDER NAME	Voldemort Savings and Loan

PMT NO	PAYMENT DATE	BEGINNING BALANCE	SCHEDULED PAYMENT	EXTRA PAYMENT	TOTAL PAYMENT	PRINCIPAL	INTEREST	ENDING BALANCE	CUMULATIVE INTEREST
1	05-06-18	$150,000.00	$716.12	$1,000.00	$1,716.12	$1,216.12	$500.00	$148,783.88	$500.00
2	05-07-18	$148,783.88	$716.12	$0.00	$716.12	$220.18	$495.95	$148,563.70	$995.95
3	05-08-18	$148,563.70	$716.12	$0.00	$716.12	$220.91	$495.21	$148,342.79	$1,491.16
4	05-09-18	$148,342.79	$716.12	$0.00	$716.12	$221.65	$494.48	$148,121.14	$1,985.63
5	05-10-18	$148,121.14	$716.12	$0.00	$716.12	$222.39	$493.74	$147,898.76	$2,479.37
6	05-11-18	$147,898.76	$716.12	$0.00	$716.12	$223.13	$493.00	$147,675.63	$2,972.37
7	05-12-18	$147,675.63	$716.12	$0.00	$716.12	$223.87	$492.25	$147,451.76	$3,464.62
8	05-01-19	$147,451.76	$716.12	$0.00	$716.12	$224.62	$491.51	$147,227.14	$3,956.13
9	05-02-19	$147,227.14	$716.12	$0.00	$716.12	$225.37	$490.76	$147,001.78	$4,446.88
10	05-03-19	$147,001.78	$716.12	$0.00	$716.12	$226.12	$490.01	$146,775.66	$4,936.89
11	05-04-19	$146,775.66	$716.12	$0.00	$716.12	$226.87	$489.25	$146,548.79	$5,426.14
12	05-05-19	$146,548.79	$716.12	$0.00	$716.12	$227.63	$488.50	$146,321.16	$5,914.64
13	05-06-19	$146,321.16	$716.12	$1,000.00	$1,716.12	$1,228.39	$487.74	$145,092.78	$6,402.37
14	05-07-19	$145,092.78	$716.12	$0.00	$716.12	$232.48	$483.64	$144,860.30	$6,886.02
15	05-08-19	$144,860.30	$716.12	$0.00	$716.12	$233.26	$482.87	$144,627.04	$7,368.88
16	05-09-19	$144,627.04	$716.12	$0.00	$716.12	$234.03	$482.09	$144,393.01	$7,850.97
17	05-10-19	$144,393.01	$716.12	$0.00	$716.12	$234.81	$481.31	$144,158.19	$8,332.28
18	05-11-19	$144,158.19	$716.12	$0.00	$716.12	$235.60	$480.53	$143,922.60	$8,812.81
19	05-12-19	$143,922.60	$716.12	$0.00	$716.12	$236.38	$479.74	$143,686.22	$9,292.55
20	05-01-20	$143,686.22	$716.12	$0.00	$716.12	$237.17	$478.95	$143,449.05	$9,771.51
21	05-02-20	$143,449.05	$716.12	$0.00	$716.12	$237.96	$478.16	$143,211.09	$10,249.67
22	05-03-20	$143,211.09	$716.12	$0.00	$716.12	$238.75	$477.37	$142,972.34	$10,727.04
23	05-04-20	$142,972.34	$716.12	$0.00	$716.12	$239.55	$476.57	$142,732.79	$11,203.62
24	05-05-20	$142,732.79	$716.12	$0.00	$716.12	$240.35	$475.78	$142,492.44	$11,679.39
25	05-06-20	$142,492.44	$716.12	$1,000.00	$1,716.12	$1,241.15	$474.97	$141,251.29	$12,154.37
26	05-07-20	$141,251.29	$716.12	$0.00	$716.12	$245.29	$470.84	$141,006.01	$12,625.20
27	05-08-20	$141,006.01	$716.12	$0.00	$716.12	$246.10	$470.02	$140,759.90	$13,095.22
28	05-09-20	$140,759.90	$716.12	$0.00	$716.12	$246.92	$469.20	$140,512.98	$13,564.42
29	05-10-20	$140,512.98	$716.12	$0.00	$716.12	$247.75	$468.38	$140,265.24	$14,032.80
30	05-11-20	$140,265.24	$716.12	$0.00	$716.12	$248.57	$467.55	$140,016.66	$14,500.35
31	05-12-20	$140,016.66	$716.12	$0.00	$716.12	$249.40	$466.72	$139,767.26	$14,967.07
32	05-01-21	$139,767.26	$716.12	$0.00	$716.12	$250.23	$465.89	$139,517.03	$15,432.96
33	05-02-21	$139,517.03	$716.12	$0.00	$716.12	$251.07	$465.06	$139,265.96	$15,898.02
34	05-03-21	$139,265.96	$716.12	$0.00	$716.12	$251.90	$464.22	$139,014.06	$16,362.24
35	05-04-21	$139,014.06	$716.12	$0.00	$716.12	$252.74	$463.38	$138,761.32	$16,825.62
36	05-05-21	$138,761.32	$716.12	$0.00	$716.12	$253.59	$462.54	$138,507.73	$17,288.16
37	05-06-21	$138,507.73	$716.12	$1,000.00	$1,716.12	$1,254.43	$461.69	$137,253.30	$17,749.85
38	05-07-21	$137,253.30	$716.12	$0.00	$716.12	$258.61	$457.51	$136,994.69	$18,207.36
39	05-08-21	$136,994.69	$716.12	$0.00	$716.12	$259.47	$456.65	$136,735.22	$18,664.01
40	05-09-21	$136,735.22	$716.12	$0.00	$716.12	$260.34	$455.78	$136,474.88	$19,119.80
41	05-10-21	$136,474.88	$716.12	$0.00	$716.12	$261.21	$454.92	$136,213.67	$19,574.71
42	05-11-21	$136,213.67	$716.12	$0.00	$716.12	$262.08	$454.05	$135,951.59	$20,028.76
43	05-12-21	$135,951.59	$716.12	$0.00	$716.12	$262.95	$453.17	$135,688.64	$20,481.93
44	05-01-22	$135,688.64	$716.12	$0.00	$716.12	$263.83	$452.30	$135,424.82	$20,934.22
45	05-02-22	$135,424.82	$716.12	$0.00	$716.12	$264.71	$451.42	$135,160.11	$21,385.64
46	05-03-22	$135,160.11	$716.12	$0.00	$716.12	$265.59	$450.53	$134,894.52	$21,836.17
47	05-04-22	$134,894.52	$716.12	$0.00	$716.12	$266.47	$449.65	$134,628.04	$22,285.82
48	05-05-22	$134,628.04	$716.12	$0.00	$716.12	$267.36	$448.76	$134,360.68	$22,734.58
49	05-06-22	$134,360.68	$716.12	$1,000.00	$1,716.12	$1,268.25	$447.87	$133,092.43	$23,182.45
50	05-07-22	$133,092.43	$716.12	$0.00	$716.12	$272.48	$443.64	$132,819.95	$23,626.09
51	05-08-22	$132,819.95	$716.12	$0.00	$716.12	$273.39	$442.73	$132,546.56	$24,068.83
52	05-09-22	$132,546.56	$716.12	$0.00	$716.12	$274.30	$441.82	$132,272.26	$24,510.65
53	05-10-22	$132,272.26	$716.12	$0.00	$716.12	$275.22	$440.91	$131,997.04	$24,951.56
54	05-11-22	$131,997.04	$716.12	$0.00	$716.12	$276.13	$439.99	$131,720.91	$25,391.55
55	05-12-22	$131,720.91	$716.12	$0.00	$716.12	$277.05	$439.07	$131,443.85	$25,830.62
56	05-01-23	$131,443.85	$716.12	$0.00	$716.12	$277.98	$438.15	$131,165.88	$26,268.76
57	05-02-23	$131,165.88	$716.12	$0.00	$716.12	$278.90	$437.22	$130,886.97	$26,705.98
58	05-03-23	$130,886.97	$716.12	$0.00	$716.12	$279.83	$436.29	$130,607.14	$27,142.27
59	05-04-23	$130,607.14	$716.12	$0.00	$716.12	$280.77	$435.36	$130,326.38	$27,577.63
60	05-05-23	$130,326.38	$716.12	$0.00	$716.12	$281.70	$434.42	$130,044.67	$28,012.05
61	05-06-23	$130,044.67	$716.12	$1,000.00	$1,716.12	$1,282.64	$433.48	$128,762.03	$28,445.53

In the mortgage we have been working with, you'll see that even if you make an extra $1,000 principal payment every year for the first five years, you still reduce your overall interest burden by $11,290.20 and your number of payments by 24, or two whole years. This is definitely worth it! I'd spend $6,000 to save $11,000 any day!

In our family, we keep a close eye out for any opportunity to pay down principal. When someone gets a freelance job: principal payment! Tax return? Principal payment! We even keep one credit card for cash rewards only. When that cash-back reward check arrives in the mail, we put it straight towards principal balance on the mortgage. That is because this is money that is not budgeted for. It is extra money. It may seem small but we do get giddy about taking $200 in cash back and using it to save money in overall interest!

The point is that every dollar counts and once you have your sight set on getting the albatross of a mortgage off your back, you'll find ways!

And what about the sister strategy to this "pay extra principal" route? That is the "make one extra payment per year" route. That works too! Consider the mortgage we've been discussing all along. Let's put an extra payment to principal at the beginning of every year and see what happens.

LOAN AMORTIZATION SCHEDULE

ENTER VALUES			LOAN SUMMARY	
Loan amount		$150,000.00	Scheduled payment	$716.12
Annual interest rate		4.00%	Scheduled number of payments	360
Loan period in years		30	Actual number of payments	310
Number of payments per year		12	Total early payments	$18,619.12
Start date of loan		05-06-18	Total interest	$90,502.51
Optional extra payments			LENDER NAME	Voldemort Savings and Loan

PMT NO	PAYMENT DATE	BEGINNING BALANCE	SCHEDULED PAYMENT	EXTRA PAYMENT	TOTAL PAYMENT	PRINCIPAL	INTEREST	ENDING BALANCE	CUMULATIVE INTEREST
1	05-06-18	$150,000.00	$716.12	$716.12	$1,432.24	$932.24	$500.00	$149,067.76	$500.00
2	05-07-18	$149,067.76	$716.12	$0.00	$716.12	$219.23	$496.89	$148,848.53	$996.89
3	05-08-18	$148,848.53	$716.12	$0.00	$716.12	$219.96	$496.16	$148,628.57	$1,493.05
4	05-09-18	$148,628.57	$716.12	$0.00	$716.12	$220.69	$495.43	$148,407.87	$1,988.48
5	05-10-18	$148,407.87	$716.12	$0.00	$716.12	$221.43	$494.69	$148,186.44	$2,483.18
6	05-11-18	$148,186.44	$716.12	$0.00	$716.12	$222.17	$493.95	$147,964.27	$2,977.13
7	05-12-18	$147,964.27	$716.12	$0.00	$716.12	$222.91	$493.21	$147,741.36	$3,470.34
8	05-01-19	$147,741.36	$716.12	$0.00	$716.12	$223.66	$492.47	$147,517.71	$3,962.82
9	05-02-19	$147,517.71	$716.12	$0.00	$716.12	$224.40	$491.73	$147,293.32	$4,454.54
10	05-03-19	$147,293.32	$716.12	$0.00	$716.12	$225.15	$490.98	$147,068.17	$4,945.52
11	05-04-19	$147,068.17	$716.12	$0.00	$716.12	$225.90	$490.23	$146,842.27	$5,435.75
12	05-05-19	$146,842.27	$716.12	$0.00	$716.12	$226.65	$489.47	$146,615.63	$5,925.22
13	05-06-19	$146,615.63	$716.12	$716.12	$1,432.24	$943.52	$488.72	$145,672.10	$6,413.94
14	05-07-19	$145,672.10	$716.12	$0.00	$716.12	$230.55	$485.57	$145,441.55	$6,899.51
15	05-08-19	$145,441.55	$716.12	$0.00	$716.12	$231.32	$484.81	$145,210.23	$7,384.32
16	05-09-19	$145,210.23	$716.12	$0.00	$716.12	$232.09	$484.03	$144,978.15	$7,868.35
17	05-10-19	$144,978.15	$716.12	$0.00	$716.12	$232.86	$483.26	$144,745.29	$8,351.61
18	05-11-19	$144,745.29	$716.12	$0.00	$716.12	$233.64	$482.49	$144,511.64	$8,834.10
19	05-12-19	$144,511.64	$716.12	$0.00	$716.12	$234.42	$481.71	$144,277.23	$9,315.80
20	05-01-20	$144,277.23	$716.12	$0.00	$716.12	$235.20	$480.92	$144,042.03	$9,796.73
21	05-02-20	$144,042.03	$716.12	$0.00	$716.12	$235.98	$480.14	$143,806.05	$10,276.87
22	05-03-20	$143,806.05	$716.12	$0.00	$716.12	$236.77	$479.35	$143,569.28	$10,756.22
23	05-04-20	$143,569.28	$716.12	$0.00	$716.12	$237.56	$478.56	$143,331.72	$11,234.78
24	05-05-20	$143,331.72	$716.12	$0.00	$716.12	$238.35	$477.77	$143,093.37	$11,712.56
25	05-06-20	$143,093.37	$716.12	$716.12	$1,432.24	$955.27	$476.98	$142,138.10	$12,189.54
26	05-07-20	$142,138.10	$716.12	$0.00	$716.12	$242.33	$473.79	$141,895.77	$12,663.33
27	05-08-20	$141,895.77	$716.12	$0.00	$716.12	$243.14	$472.99	$141,652.64	$13,136.31
28	05-09-20	$141,652.64	$716.12	$0.00	$716.12	$243.95	$472.18	$141,408.69	$13,608.49
29	05-10-20	$141,408.69	$716.12	$0.00	$716.12	$244.76	$471.36	$141,163.93	$14,079.85
30	05-11-20	$141,163.93	$716.12	$0.00	$716.12	$245.58	$470.55	$140,918.35	$14,550.40
31	05-12-20	$140,918.35	$716.12	$0.00	$716.12	$246.40	$469.73	$140,671.96	$15,020.13
32	05-01-21	$140,671.96	$716.12	$0.00	$716.12	$247.22	$468.91	$140,424.74	$15,489.03
33	05-02-21	$140,424.74	$716.12	$0.00	$716.12	$248.04	$468.08	$140,176.70	$15,957.12
34	05-03-21	$140,176.70	$716.12	$0.00	$716.12	$248.87	$467.26	$139,927.83	$16,424.37
35	05-04-21	$139,927.83	$716.12	$0.00	$716.12	$249.70	$466.43	$139,678.13	$16,890.80
36	05-05-21	$139,678.13	$716.12	$0.00	$716.12	$250.53	$465.59	$139,427.61	$17,356.39
37	05-06-21	$139,427.61	$716.12	$716.12	$1,432.24	$967.48	$464.76	$138,460.12	$17,821.15
38	05-07-21	$138,460.12	$716.12	$0.00	$716.12	$254.59	$461.53	$138,205.53	$18,282.68
39	05-08-21	$138,205.53	$716.12	$0.00	$716.12	$255.44	$460.69	$137,950.09	$18,743.37
40	05-09-21	$137,950.09	$716.12	$0.00	$716.12	$256.29	$459.83	$137,693.80	$19,203.20
41	05-10-21	$137,693.80	$716.12	$0.00	$716.12	$257.14	$458.98	$137,436.66	$19,662.18
42	05-11-21	$137,436.66	$716.12	$0.00	$716.12	$258.00	$458.12	$137,178.66	$20,120.30
43	05-12-21	$137,178.66	$716.12	$0.00	$716.12	$258.86	$457.26	$136,919.80	$20,577.57
44	05-01-22	$136,919.80	$716.12	$0.00	$716.12	$259.72	$456.40	$136,660.08	$21,033.97
45	05-02-22	$136,660.08	$716.12	$0.00	$716.12	$260.59	$455.53	$136,399.49	$21,489.50
46	05-03-22	$136,399.49	$716.12	$0.00	$716.12	$261.46	$454.66	$136,138.03	$21,944.16
47	05-04-22	$136,138.03	$716.12	$0.00	$716.12	$262.33	$453.79	$135,875.70	$22,397.96
48	05-05-22	$135,875.70	$716.12	$0.00	$716.12	$263.20	$452.92	$135,612.50	$22,850.88
49	05-06-22	$135,612.50	$716.12	$716.12	$1,432.24	$980.20	$452.04	$134,632.29	$23,302.92
50	05-07-22	$134,632.29	$716.12	$0.00	$716.12	$267.35	$448.77	$134,364.95	$23,751.69
51	05-08-22	$134,364.95	$716.12	$0.00	$716.12	$268.24	$447.88	$134,096.71	$24,199.58
52	05-09-22	$134,096.71	$716.12	$0.00	$716.12	$269.13	$446.99	$133,827.57	$24,646.56
53	05-10-22	$133,827.57	$716.12	$0.00	$716.12	$270.03	$446.09	$133,557.54	$25,092.66
54	05-11-22	$133,557.54	$716.12	$0.00	$716.12	$270.93	$445.19	$133,286.61	$25,537.85
55	05-12-22	$133,286.61	$716.12	$0.00	$716.12	$271.83	$444.29	$133,014.79	$25,982.14
56	05-01-23	$133,014.79	$716.12	$0.00	$716.12	$272.74	$443.38	$132,742.03	$26,425.52
57	05-02-23	$132,742.03	$716.12	$0.00	$716.12	$273.65	$442.47	$132,468.39	$26,867.99
58	05-03-23	$132,468.39	$716.12	$0.00	$716.12	$274.56	$441.56	$132,193.82	$27,309.55
59	05-04-23	$132,193.82	$716.12	$0.00	$716.12	$275.48	$440.65	$131,918.35	$27,750.20
60	05-05-23	$131,918.35	$716.12	$0.00	$716.12	$276.40	$439.73	$131,641.95	$28,189.93
61	05-06-23	$131,641.95	$716.12	$716.12	$1,432.24	$993.44	$438.81	$130,648.52	$28,628.73
62	05-07-23	$130,648.52	$716.12	$0.00	$716.12	$280.63	$435.50	$130,367.89	$29,064.23
63	05-08-23	$130,367.89	$716.12	$0.00	$716.12	$281.56	$434.56	$130,086.32	$29,498.79
64	05-09-23	$130,086.32	$716.12	$0.00	$716.12	$282.50	$433.62	$129,803.82	$29,932.41
65	05-10-23	$129,803.82	$716.12	$0.00	$716.12	$283.44	$432.68	$129,520.38	$30,365.09
66	05-11-23	$129,520.38	$716.12	$0.00	$716.12	$284.39	$431.73	$129,235.99	$30,796.82
67	05-12-23	$129,235.99	$716.12	$0.00	$716.12	$285.34	$430.79	$128,950.65	$31,227.61
68	05-01-24	$128,950.65	$716.12	$0.00	$716.12	$286.29	$429.84	$128,664.37	$31,657.45

If you make just one extra payment to principal on this loan, you will save yourself 50 payments which amounts to over four years. You will also save yourself $17,301.75 in interest overall which is nothing to shake a stick at! Is it as gratifying as those big whacks of cash at principal we talked about earlier? No because you are only attacking Public Enemy #1: Interest. You are not attacking Public Enemy #2: Time. But you are still in attack mode so it counts!

And a point of personal privilege here: we have found that when we set our sights on these amortization charts, we find a way to attack them that may not have been in our budget. We believe that when you put your intention on your wealth consciousness, the universe gets on board. Call it a "DO Pass Go and DO Collect $200" bonus. These things happen when you set your intention towards them. We are willing to bet that you'll find unexpected principal payments coming your way once you've set your sights on them. If we are right, please write us and let us know how!

6
Conclusion

THE STRATEGIES DISCUSSED in this book are not for everyone. In fact, most people will not do this because, in the immortal words of Jim Rohn: "What's easy to do is easier not to do." But if you are serious about living financially free, you will find a way to implement at least some of the tools discussed.

We know that part of your motivation to do this is your love of your home.

We get that, we love our home too. But your home

is not a Performing Asset and funneling most of your money into it every month is not a wealth-building strategy.

Basic business accounting tells us that the purpose of an asset is to produce cash flow. The purpose of a liability is to buy an asset that produces cash flow. By that definition, your home is not an asset.

"Oh but my home is appreciating in value," you may say. To which we ask, "Can you pay your bills with that appreciation? Can you eat it? Do you plan to retire on that appreciation? What are you DOING with that appreciation?"

Crickets.....

Appreciation is a concept you use to make yourself feel better about an expensive liability. But even if you plan to benefit from this appreciation by selling your house for more money than you bought it for, that is still a single transactional event. It is one pile of cash like your 401(k) cash-out. That is not a stream of cash you can live off of. That is a lump sum that will be taxed and is over and done with. Then you will have to figure out how long you can make that money last.

No. Your home does not cash flow. Your home cash sucks.

For most of us, a primary mortgage is our largest liability. It is our budget. It is the thing that keeps us needing regular streams of cash flow to afford. It is the liability we have strapped to ourselves like ankle weights. It is often the liability that we use to shape our entire lives.

Can we afford this mortgage? Then we can afford to live here and we'll decide what else we can afford based on this mortgage.

The problem with that line of thinking is that it means little to none of your income is going towards buying Performing Assets! A Performing Asset is an asset that pays you every month like a business you own or invest in, or a piece of real estate that you can rent out. Wealthy people invest in Performing Assets for cash flow. The rest invest in liabilities for just the opposite. When all of your cash is sunk into a non-Performing Asset such as a mortgage, there is no wealth building. There is only treading water.

Tom Wheelwright, our super duper CPA mentioned in previous chapters, offers this simple solution to liabilities attached to non-performing assets:

"If you have a liability for something that does not produce cash flow, you either sell that asset or pay off the liability."

That is basically what we have been getting at this entire book! Sure you can sell your home and move into something without a mortgage. You could rent something cheaper. Or you can accelerate your mortgage payoff so that you free up your cash to start actually buying Performing Assets. Only then will you really be wealth building!

We get that home ownership is a central storyline to the American Dream. But we do not overly romanticize this to the point that we are willing to overpay for our home over the course of 30 years. We will not let our primary mortgage be the number one driver of our lifestyle. We want out of this expensive liability as quickly as possible because we USE our equity to make investments all the time! We actively plan to break the mold of primary mortgage slavery and we have done it, time and again.

So here is what we challenge you to do: take a good hard look at your primary mortgage liability and think about how is attached to an asset that does not perform. Think about how you can shift your cash flow in your house away from non-Performing Assets and towards Performing Assets. After all, as the ever-so-blunt Robert Kiyosaki says:

"The rich buy assets. The poor buy liabilities."

Which one are you aiming for?

Celebrate Good Times

W**E WOULD LIKE TO CONCLUDE** by affirming that this strategy works! We paid off a mortgage with a $294,000 balance in less than two years with this strategy. We opened a very expensive bottle of wine to celebrate! We'd love for you to be able to do the same.

Now go forth, pay off that mortgage! And write to us about your credit card vacation and mortgage payoff wine so that we toast to you in our home too! We are always on the lookout for excuses to toast something!

Thank You

WE WANT TO THANK YOU for reading this book. Even if you never employ these strategies, we at least hope that this book has armed you with tools to better understand your home mortgage and personal finances in order to make better decisions at every turn. But of course we want you to be mortgage-free. We want you to use your money to build wealth, not pay down debt. We want you to thrive, not survive!

On our website, www.morrisinvest.com, we have blogs, videos, and podcasts about how to build wealth and live off of passive income in order to be truly free from the rat race. Being free of a mortgage is just one step towards financial freedom. Having monthly cash flow is another. We help investors learn to buy Performing Assets. We help investors buy rental real estate and learn to set up their estates so that they can build legacy wealth for themselves and their families. We hope you will explore our content because we spend a lot of time making it to inspire other families like ours! Best of luck to you and yours from us and ours!

APPENDIX

Next Steps

Now that you're done with this book, here are some next steps for you.

1. JOIN THE COMMUNITY

Clayton and Natali are proud to announce the launch of our Financial Freedom Academy. If you are serious about taking control of your finances and ready to build financial freedom we invite you to join us here:

www.FinancialFreedomAcademy.com

2. SUBSCRIBE TO OUR PODCAST.

Our Investing in Real Estate Podcast is available on iTunes. We teach you how to build wealth through real estate. Here's the link:

www.ClaytonMorris.com

3. VISIT OUR YOUTUBE CHANNEL.

Each week we publish videos to help you create financial intelligence. We have an entire series devoted to creating passive income. Check it out and subscribe for free right here:

www.youtube.com/morrisinvest

4. SHARE THIS BOOK

Please write a review on Amazon and tell others who you think will enjoy this book. Spreading the word helps to reach new readers, grow this movement, and continue to produce similar content. Also if you haven't yet read our other titles, now would be a good time to take a look.

bit.ly/DebtFreeMortgage

THANK YOU!

Printed in Great Britain
by Amazon